Y0-BBD-651

Essential Question
In what ways do people show they care
about each other?

SAVING STOLEN TREASURE

by Eve Tonkin • illustrated by Merrill Rainey

Chapter 1

PLAY PRACTICE

It was Friday afternoon, and play practice wasn't going well. Ms. Anderson was worn out. Kids **whirled** around the room. Other kids **expressed** their ideas about the play, but no one could agree on which ones to use.

"We have two weeks until our performance for your families!" Ms. Anderson said. "King Cris, stop arguing with Queen Chelsea! Sam, stop that monkey noise. You are *not* going to be the monkey in the play!"

Ms. Anderson took a breath and continued, "We *must* decide by Monday what the **treasure** is going to be. Will the treasure be Spanish gold or jewelry?" A few kids started talking. "This is serious, class. Our play *Stolen Treasure* is in trouble!"

The class was silent, and then Ms. Anderson smiled. "Things will be better on Monday," she said. "I hope everyone has a good weekend. I know I will! I'm going dancing with my husband on Saturday."

On Monday, the class was surprised to see Mr. Kowalski, a **substitute** teacher, in the classroom. "Ms. Anderson broke her leg dancing," he said.

"Oh, no!" Erica exclaimed. "When will she be back?"

"I don't know," Mr. Kowalski said. "But we do need to get started with play practice."

Rani muttered, "I hope I don't have to wear that stupid hat."

"You have to wear the hat," Violet said. "Don't be **fussy**."

"Ms. Anderson says you need to decide on the treasure," said Mr. Kowalski. "What will it be?"

"Jewelry!" shouted several kids.

"Spanish coins!" said others.

Mr. Kowalski said, "I'll need to ask Ms. Anderson."

Chelsea whispered to Erica, "We're wasting **precious** time."

Erica looked at the class **portraits** on the wall. Ms. Anderson had taken the photos on a class trip. "We need some **advice**. Let's visit Ms. Anderson after school and ask for help."

STOP AND CHECK

Why does the class have a substitute teacher?

Chapter 2

WORKING TOGETHER

The next day after school, Erica and Chelsea went to see Ms. Anderson. Ms. Anderson was Erica's neighbor.

"How is Ms. Anderson?" Erica asked when Mr. Anderson opened the door.

"She's worried because Mr. Kowalski says the play isn't going well," Mr. Anderson said.

"We can't do it without her," Chelsea replied.

"Unfortunately, you'll have to," Mr. Anderson said. "She won't be back at school for a few months."

"Can we please see her?" Chelsea asked.

"Yes. I'll tell her you're here," Mr. Anderson said.

"We can't ask Ms. Anderson for advice now," Erica whispered to Chelsea as soon as he had gone. "We need to cheer her up, not make her more worried!"

When the girls went in to see Ms. Anderson, it was strange to see her leg covered in a plaster cast and piled high on pillows.

"Don't look so worried," Ms. Anderson said to the girls. "I'm enjoying the rest. How is everything at school?"

"Play practice was hard at first, but it's getting better," Erica said.

Ms. Anderson said, "That's great news!"

STOP AND CHECK

Why don't the girls ask Ms. Anderson for help?

The next day in class, Mr. Kowalski announced, "Erica and Chelsea have something to say."

"We visited Ms. Anderson yesterday," Erica said. "She won't be coming back to school for a few months."

Everyone started talking at once.

"How big is her cast?" called Sam.

"It's huge," said Chelsea. "Her whole leg is in a cast."

Michael asked, "Are we still going to do the play?"

"That's what we need to talk about," said Erica firmly.

Erica continued, "Ms. Anderson wants us to do a good job with the play, and she's worried we can't do it without her."

"That's probably because we keep arguing," said Michael.

"We have to work together and listen to one another," Erica said. "We need to make this play **awesome** for Ms. Anderson!"

"Does everyone agree with Erica?" Michael asked.

Everyone raised their hands.

"Great!" Erica said. "Which part of the play should we work on first?"

Violet said, "For a start, Sam can be the king's tiger, *not* a monkey."

Sam nodded.

"I have an idea about the treasure," said Jaden. "We could have coins and jewelry. Then we all get what we want."

"Yes!" everyone replied together.

"Let's add that into the play right now," Violet said. "Then the writing will be finished."

"That's a good idea," Mr. Kowalski said.

STOP AND CHECK

Why do the two girls take over running the class play?

Chapter 3

OPENING NIGHT

On opening night, Ms. Anderson couldn't wait to see the play. Erica and Mr. Kowalski told her that the class was working well together.

Ms. Anderson whispered to Mr. Anderson, "Could you please go backstage? Tell the class they don't have to break a leg because I already did it. Their success is **guaranteed**!"

Mr. Anderson nodded, and he gave Ms. Anderson the thumbs-up when he got back.

The lights dimmed, and the play began.

The class had a fantastic time onstage. They had created a **magnificent** play by listening to each other's ideas.

They had fun working together, too. King Cris and Queen Chelsea stopped fighting, and Erica helped Sam get ready for his role as a tiger.

Best of all, the treasure of Spanish gold and jewelry worked perfectly. It **sparkled** in the bright stage lights.

The people in the audience clapped loudly when the play ended, and the class took a bow. Then Erica gave a signal, and the class chanted, "Ms. An-der-son! Ms. An-der-son!"

Mr. Anderson helped his surprised wife onto the stage. The class **encircled** her, and Chelsea gave her a **bouquet** of flowers.

Ms. Anderson spoke into the microphone. Her voice was full of **emotion**. "I'm so proud of my wonderful class. They wrote the play, and they worked together so well! Even after I broke my leg!"

Everyone smiled, and the audience clapped. The **applause** was even louder this time!

STOP AND CHECK

Why did the class call Ms. Anderson up onto the stage?

Respond to Reading

Summarize

Use details from the text to summarize how the class saved the play. Your graphic organizer may help you.

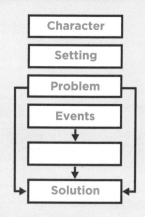

Character

Setting

Problem

Events

Solution

Text Evidence

1. Reread Chapter 1. What problem does the class have with the play? **PROBLEM AND SOLUTION**

2. Find the word *cast* on page 7. What does it mean? What clues in the text helped you figure out the meaning? **VOCABULARY**

3. Write about how Erica and Chelsea solved the problem in the story. **WRITE ABOUT READING**

Compare Texts

Read about a boy who helped his sister overcome her shyness.

Miguel's Amazing Shyness Cure

Miguel tossed the basketball into the hoop.

"Miguel, your sister's here again," Cody called.

Jade stood at the side of the basketball court. She looked sad.

Miguel walked over to her. "Why aren't you playing with the kids in your class?" he asked gently.

Jade didn't reply.

Miguel knew that it was hard for Jade at school because she was shy, but he also felt annoyed. She hung around him all the time. "I'll walk you back to class," he said.

Jade gave Miguel a picture when they met at the front gate after school. "We had to draw our best friend. I drew a picture of you playing basketball."

Miguel smiled at her. "It's awesome, Jade," he said.

Back at home, Miguel thought about Jade's problem. "I wish I could give her something to cure her shyness," he thought.

Suddenly he had an idea!

Illustration: Joanne Renaud

At dinner, Miguel made an announcement, "Jade gave me a drawing today, so I have something for her."

He gave Jade a box with MIGUEL'S AMAZING SHYNESS CURE written on it.

Jade opened the lid. Miguel's favorite crystal lay inside.

"It helped me when I was shy. You take a deep breath and squeeze it when you feel that way," Miguel said. "Then your shyness goes away."

"Wow!" Jade's eyes were shining. She said, "Thanks, Miguel. I'll try it tomorrow!"

Make Connections

How do Miguel's actions show that he cares about his sister? ESSENTIAL QUESTION

How are Erica in *Saving Stolen Treasure* and Miguel in *Miguel's Amazing Shyness Cure* alike? TEXT TO TEXT

Illustration: Joanne Renaud

Focus on Genre

Realistic Fiction Realistic fiction tells a story that could take place in real life. Writers use characters and settings that are believable. The characters have the same kinds of problems that real people might have.

Read and Find Erica has a problem in *Saving Stolen Treasure*. She wants to get the class to work together. Why does this problem seem believable? Miguel's little sister in *Miguel's Amazing Shyness Cure* is too shy to make friends. Why does this problem seem believable?

Your Turn

Choose a character from either story. Then think of another problem the character might have. What would you do if you were that person? Work with a partner. Talk about the character you chose. How would you solve the character's problem?